Safe Hands

Recover your Well-being Through Creativity And Play

Nikki Weston

Print ISBN: 978-1-9162783-1-8

Published by: Nicola McKenna

Cover Designs by: Nicola McKenna

Copywriter: Nicola McKenna

DEDICATION

To Jamie and Nicholas,

for teaching me how to play

CONTENTS

ACKNOWLEDGEMENTS

Thanks go to the many kind and generous writers and artists who have given me their time, wisdom, and friendship over the years. You prove every day that this stuff works.

I would like to acknowledge the works of writers and teachers Julia Cameron, Steven Pressfield, and Anne McDonald, whose concepts and materials have shaped the ways in which I think and see the world.

I thank the workshop attendees and those who have expressed an interest in what I'm attempting to achieve with this book, your enthusiasm means the world to me.

I am grateful for the read and constant enthusiasm from my sister and greatest cheerleader Elaine Coomber; my friend Anne McDonald for so much plus a blurb; my writing coach Irene S. Roth; my sister-in-kind Sia Huff; Sarah Godwin for priceless Mondays and Fridays; Jackie Jarvis for the jolt; Suzette Tackney for narrating all those years ago and in more recent times her support of this book; Elaine Murphy for the tea, advice, and runs to Balbriggan; Katie Wink for the job offer; Clare McLoughlin for the copious advice on cover and design, and Paddy in Skerries Bookshop for more of the same.

For their constant support and enthusiasm, I thank my Clones friends; my Dublin friends especially the RaLET parents and staff;

my writer friends in Mag7FD and Romance Writers of America; my incredible Carney inlaws; Mam and Dad for literally everything; Carol-Ann, Elaine, Amby, Dec, Siobhán, Gerry, their partners and children.
Finally, I thank Alan. Mostly for eating my burnt dinners night after night and saying they're lovely.

1 INTRODUCTION

Welcome to *Safe Hands*, a short guide to discovering your creativity and seeing what it can do for you.

Safe Hands is neither a writer's book nor an artist's book. It is an 'everyone' book. It doesn't require skills or talents. It is part workbook, part confessional, part minder. It is intended for you and your creative outlet, whether that exists yet or not.

Safe Hands is your first step in getting space and time to yourself. What I call small lil baby space; teeny-tiny time. Both of these will help your happiness and mental health.

At its most basic, *Safe Hands* is about keeping the hands busy on small simple stuff so that the mind can switch off. It is about making and doing using everyday things around us, crafting the quick inexpensive way, and playing silly for a while, giving us the headspace we need.

Safe Hands is designed to fight pretence. It is designed to stand up to perfect. It doesn't need you to state your age, gender, or occupation. It doesn't care what you did before today.

While some creative outlets feel weird, others feel natural and right. *Safe Hands* helps you think about what type of creativity is natural and right for you. We'll do some activities, have a bit of fun, and take it from there.

My approach in this book is kind, honest, and realistic. I will give you mistakes, not ideals. I have only minutes, not days, so this book is short and can be read either straight through, or dipped into now and then.

There are three parts: Thinking, Feeling, and Doing.

'Part One: Thinking' looks at not changing your life (I'll explain later). It examines your life as it is today. It asks you to think about figuring out your creative thing: there are questions to remind you what creative pursuits you did in the past, and consider what you might like to do in the future. Finally, it looks at what stops us from taking time out for ourselves.

'Part Two: Feeling' gets into fear. It talks about the whisper of ideas and the roaring that follows. It introduces Resistance. It deals with failure, permission, doing things badly. It deals with distractions, both good and bad. It shares the fears of artistic people who've been there, and one or two confessions from yours truly.

'Part Three: Doing' describes the 'how' of creative recovery. It talks about minding the gap - that chasm of fear that can threaten your first creative step. It talks about compassion and how we treat ourselves. It reassures, showing us others who have found their creative sides safely and easily.

Finally, section 37 'Safe Dates', at the very end of this book, gives you oodles of easy ways to make time for yourself that don't take all day or decimate your debit card. Feel free to turn to this section whenever you feel like you need space, and do that activity. I promise you, it's magic.

While I'm inspired by the work of teachers Julia Cameron and Steven Pressfield, I mostly pull from my own living and trying, my own failings and triumphs. I'm still working on it and I probably always will.

2 DISCLAIMER

I am not the Dalai Lama ('SURPRISE!'). I am not a guru. I am not a philanthropist or a philosopher. I am not on a pedestal. I am not backed by a board room of investors.

I am not a doctor of any sort. A traditional publisher would probably force me to put in some kind of disclaimer, but since I'm publishing solo, I'll do it My Way:

"A friendly neighbourhood reminder that should you have a serious issue of the head or heart, talk to someone who will listen or consult a professional, be that a psychologist, a cardiac surgeon, or anything in between."

You will not find quotes from leaders or pioneers. You will not find Instagrammable mantras. You will not find attempts to inspire or aspire.

You will find UK English, UK punctuation, and many Irishisms such as 'the doing' and 'rake' (rake = butt load). While I understand that North American punctuation should be inside single quotes marks (and not outside), please know that I had to choose one style so I went with the UK English that we use here in Ireland. If you simply cannot stand to read punctuation that's not tailored to your geographical location, I humbly apologise.

You will find honesty and vulnerability and fear and a rake (butt load!) of other things. You'll find ways to play. You'll find permission, encouragement to make a mess, and even more encouragement to make mistakes. And the closest thing we get to celebrity is the Brothers Franco in 'The Disaster Artist'.

You might think that being creative is easy for me. You could think that because I wrote the book, I have all the answers.

Alas, I do not have the answers ('because the answers are inside you...' So that's kinda sorta Dalai Lama-ish). I'll be upfront with you and say that this book is not prescriptive. It's not some recipe for happiness or a manual to 'change your life'.

It's small, safe stuff I've found useful in getting myself and other people back to creativity, and in so doing, reaching what feels like a content life.

I reckon we could all do with that.

3 MY RECOVERY

I am Nicola McKenna writing as Nikki Weston, and I live in Dublin, Ireland.

All my life, I told myself what I was: good, hardworking, intelligent, upright, pleasant, helpful, ordinary, uncomplicated, reliable, everyday.

Art and creativity was not a big part of my upbringing. Art has always felt like an indulgence. Writing has always appeared to me to be high-brow, staunchly regulated, or snobbish.

Creativity felt unattainable, and notably, the complete opposite of productive. It seems suited to others: people who are either ballsy, or reckless, or blessed with an unmistakeable talent that is a sin not to use. In other words, not me.

Now, I have always enjoyed reading and writing. The sound of a word can distract me from whatever I'm doing; thinking about irregular past participles still causes me to flush with excitement.

At some point in my childhood, I decided I wanted to write for a living. But the writers I learned about had problems. Big scary problems. They were alcoholic, they were broke, or their wild lifestyle made them unsavoury. They were either put on a pedestal, or were dying in gutters. They didn't live in ordinary families like mine, in ordinary towns like mine. They wrote depressing verse and dark stories. Writers, artists, actors, musicians. They were ego-filled or misunderstood. They were written off or mentally ill.

Somewhere along the line, I picked up the belief that writers were born, not made, and that I was not one of the chosen ones. On one hand, it meant I didn't have any talent, but on the other, I would never die starving under a bridge.

Besides, there was, as there probably still is, a push from society urging me to 'be something', for academic success and financial independence, of joining the workforce and seeing the world.

Add this to a painfully thin skin and a young girl's need for society's approval. As a result, I worked hard to get a good job. I wrote off the possibility of pursuing my real goal: writing for a living. I believed this for thirty-odd years.

Until I heard of Julia Cameron's book 'The Artist's Way', a 12-week program to help people discover creativity lost or blocked or never discovered. I found a supportive facilitator, and in a small group, I did the full program twice over two years.

In that time, I kept living my life, working and raising my kids, burning the dinner. Same sh!t, different day.

But things were on the move. In the supermarket, I'd pick up some coloured cardboard for a euro or two. The next month, my kids brought home some cool gel pens. Momma here 'borrowed' those. Once when I was buying schoolbooks, I saw a big bottle of PVA crafting glue for next to nothing, and I added it to the bill.

In time, I had myself a little craft box. Odds and ends, spare buttons, ribbons from gift wrapping. Pretty coloured cellophane from a floral bouquet or an eye-catching greeting card. Things that appealed to me ended up in the shoe box that I called my 'craft box.

I started to use the stuff in it. When I'd burn the dinner or a kid had a meltdown, I'd recover as best I could and as soon as there were 10 minutes free, I would pull out the craft box. I might cut up the pages of an old magazine, glue-stick the wonky shapes onto the coloured card. Any old way. I just kept pasting until the card was entirely covered. I told myself it wasn't important the how or the why. For ten minutes, because my hands were busy playing, my brain didn't care enough to obsess about that or about anything. It was a total switch off.

If a massive bill came through the letter box, typically I fumed my way through the best part of a week until I could take it no longer. I would feel the need for some time to myself, so I took off for an hour with a legal pad, a few pencils, and doodled. Playing with shading, or making a really awful sketch — it didn't matter. What mattered was it was switch-off time; distraction from the big scary bill. I had given myself a little kindness, a little time. For a tiny fraction of the day, I had put myself first. I hadn't splurged on a new anything in order to help me forget. I hadn't drunk my anger away. I hadn't hurt anyone; my actions hadn't made matters worse. The big scary bill was still there when I got home, but I was less angry.

Ironically, I felt I could handle the big and the scary.

I had finished the The Artist's Way months before. It is sized at twelve weeks, so it's not quick. I wasn't reading it again or doing any of the exercises. But something was changing.

Did I do something big? Did I (clears throat) Change My Life?

Hell, no.

I was seeking balance, not in a 50% work 50% life way, and not in a perfect way. More like 0.005% time to myself and completely imperfect. In other words, a little space to make mistakes. I sensed the help that making stuff brought to my life. I felt I was in safe hands, and when I looked down, I was shocked to find those hands were mine.

I started to like minding myself that tiny little bit. I felt the difference. I started taking time to make, craft, and experiment, more often.

My life was still organised chaos - our kids still went bananas ten times a day and, as a family, we still had all manner of problems. No one on the outside saw anything radical or revolutionary. But inside things were a little easier. I felt a little lighter. I went about carving time to myself once a week, and was surprised to find that no one was forgotten or abandoned or burned alive. Small wee pockets of time that were so teeny tiny, so easy and pleasurable, so distracting and relaxing, that I thought it miraculous. At the very least, I presumed it was an idea that lots of other people knew and used.

In early 2018, I taught an Artist's Way class for a friend. Some attendees managed to make it, others didn't. I liked the ideas of self-care, using crafting to get away from it all, and artist dates. But living that way isn't easy for a lot of people, myself included. Time is limited, and people are busy with families, jobs, and lives. So I wanted to find a way of moulding all this into everyday life, for everyday people.

I wrote the first version of this book, and in late 2018, I taught it as a workshop. I found I was good at listening, asking a question or two, cheering successes small and big. The class attendees could see breakthroughs, possibilities, paths they might take, feelings of lightness.

Everyone outside of these circles however still had the same problems. I would mention creativity as a potential solution, but the idea was often met with disbelief or horror. Most thought it was only suitable to those who 'identify' as an artist, or a writer, or a musician. No one entertained the possibility that creativity took many forms and could be used to help oneself.

From what I can see, creativity is misunderstood, undervalued, and underused. I believe it gives much more than it takes. I believe in breaking down misconceptions about who is creative and why.

I'm writing this book because I believe others need to hear about this. I have seen the worth in myself, a regular everyday person, and in my creations. I have seen other everyday people see the worth in themselves and their creations. When someone makes something and feels good about it, I clap like a seal at feeding time. That's when I knew I wanted to write this book.

Hands up, who's scared? Who wants to quit this creativity lark and hit YouTube for some crazy cat videos? I hear you, but first, let's chat.

4 (DON'T) CHANGE YOUR LIFE

Okay, so that's a dig at self-help books. So many people claim that following their books can do just that: change your life.

I take issue with this claim. The phrase alone suggests effort, and lots of it. It suggests 'work' and 'busy' and 'schedules' and 'efficient'. It conjures up plans and goals and progress.

See what I mean? Terrifying.

I sense in it a promise. Some brand of 180-degree magic. A turnaround from crap to cool. From fail to fab. I also sense they're lying. I hear 'change your life' and think of calling the folks in charge of the Trade Descriptions Act.

What we are doing in Safe Hands is making space to explore one or two small creative outlets. Not changing big stuff in our lives. Not ditching families or travelling the world. Not changing your religion or joining the Peace Corps.

The funny thing is, proportionally speaking, a small change makes a big difference. You're happier with that small bit of creativity, be it decaling stuff onto wooden furniture, pinging on a keyboard or painting a mediocre watercolour, than with a complete life overhaul (which sounds utterly exhausting).

Taking the first step is safer than you think. It's small and kind like a cuddly bear. Doing creative stuff won't drain you. It doesn't attack your integrity or your sense of self. It won't suck up all oxygen in the immediate vicinity. It won't cause your spouse to leave you, it won't lose you money, and it won't force you to eat pitying insults from 'concerned' friends.

So please, don't change your life. That's way too scary.

Stick with me for an hour or so, think a while about what pleases you, what you daydream about, what your goals were before life sucker-punched you. Write it down or use my handy Activities print-off if you want to. In time, you might take a step. Or you might not. Either option is cool. You are safe here, you are supported, and no matter what you do in the next fifty pages, the world will keep turning. I promise.

If you've got the fear, I do too. If you have responsibilities, meet your sister. If you believe it can't be done, please bear with me.

The activities in this e-book will gently unlock the door just enough to let you in. Think about what you want to create. Permit yourself to speak up. Make a mess, make a mistake or two. You're in safe hands.

NOTES ON THIS CHAPTER:

First: My personal opinion is that many self-help books are well-marketed rubbish, promising a quick-fix and pouncing on our vulnerabilities. The really bad ones make us feel even more crap than we did before. Marianne Power, a UK-based journalist, wrote the hilarious book 'Help Me!' (Picador, 2018) about her quest to see if self-help really could change her life. I loved this book.

Second: For readers who, like me, can't bring themselves to write on books, you'll find all the activities from this book in one handy *Safe Hands* workbook. Go to my website: www.nikkiweston.com/safe-hands-the-book and scroll down to find this free printable workbook in .doc or .pdf format. Jot down your thoughts to each *Safe Hands* activity and keep them all in one place.

PART ONE: THINKING

'Everyone Matters'
   MEMOIR BY MARY ROBINSON
   CHAIR OF THE ELDERS

5 WHAT CREATIVE RECOVERY IS (AND ISN'T)

For generations, people the world over have shown that doing creative stuff helps them. It helps them mentally, emotionally, and often spiritually and physically. I agree, and am passionate about helping others see the possibilities of this simple and easy life tool.

Being creative is not about being 'good at' something. It's not about the something at the end, the thing you point at saying "I made that". Creativity is about the enjoyment you get from making it. It's about the process you put yourself through in order to create it. It's the making, the doing.

Creative outlets don't have to be elite or high-brow or perfect. In fact, they're better when they're normal, expected, everyday pleasures, carried out with kindness, compassion, and fun. Creativity is in all of us, even you, but it means different things to different people.

Your creative outlet might be crochet, or photography, or writing, amateur dramatics, or doodling. It might be baking or poetry or rapping or needlepoint. It might be learning the mouth organ. It might be building huge statues from tiny pebbles, making Russian dolls out of buttons, or making sea glass art. It might be designing a new video game or shaping your garden hedge into a Mohican.

Whatever.

As long as it makes you happy.

Not masterful. Not famous. Not perfect.

6 MYTHS ABOUT CREATIVITY

This book was going to be subtitled 'Creative recovery for the lost, exhausted, or overwhelmed'. And then I realised that describes almost everyone I know. Including myself.

No one's perfect, and no one knows it all, but we've seen people using creative activities as outlets for fun, for profit, to record memories, to lessen stress, to switch off for a while, to find inspiration or even a first step in trying something bigger. We've learned that it's cheap, easy, and accessible.

So why are there still so many myths around being creative? Things like:

- Being creative wastes all your spare time.

- It is selfish and indulgent.

- Creative goals take forever to obtain.

- They demand lots and lots of money.

- They will leave you broke, broken, mentally unstable.

- The creative process opens up painful wounds.

- Creative pursuit means you must be melodramatic, overly

sensitive, self-obsessed.

- Life can be only practical or only creative, and never the twain shall meet.

- Creative outlets are only for those with no responsibilities and therefore have nothing better to do.

- Creative pursuits are fraught with difficulties and failures and rejections.

- There is a small and limited amount of creative success to go round.

Let's answer the charges.

It doesn't take up much time. Creative recovery relies heavily on our everyday reality: 'What resources like money, expertise and time do I actually have? How can I get the biggest bang for my buck?'

Instead of wasting time, creating stuff gives us energy. It's ironic and mysterious, but somehow when we carve out time for ourselves, we become stronger for others. Once we feed our needs, it's as if we are then allowed back into the race, allowed to do those essential things that demand so much of us. We are better able to continue caring for the things in life that matter to us.

Creative recovery doesn't break what's already good in our lives. It is rarely dramatic, it is best minus pretence, it doesn't need to be loud or high-fallutin'.

It won't make you lose your family, your money, or your mind.

It heals that darker part of you that secretly believes this whole creative outlet lark is stupid and dumb and a huge waste of time.

It does not stop the world from turning.

Crucially, creative recovery is about reclaiming a small bit of what was once a part of us. Creativity is one of life's foodstuffs. It feeds the part of us that believes our time is better spent doing something else, doing something 'more useful'. It hugs the part of us that we chastise, our only crime being that we are serving ourselves first.

It is easy but it involves crossing a bridge or two (but isn't that why you're reading this? ;-))

7 BUT WHAT'S THE POINT?

Often when we start something new, a question flies around like a mosquito, wanting to know what it is that you plan on doing with your thing.

"Are you going to sell all these sweaters that you knit?"

"Wow, you're writing a book! Have you got a publisher?"

"So you want to act. Great. Of course, you know you'll have to move to LA immediately?"

At the time, questions like these appear to be important. They can come from the people around us, but mostly they come from ourselves.

They are posed with urgency, concern, the need to know, to understand the motivation behind such a crazy idea. To look into the future and evaluate whether this venture is worthwhile or just an ego-fuelled folly.

These questions are akin to saying 'what's the point?' Beware of these three little words. 'What's the point...' is something that kills ideas before they've begun.

'What's the point…' is too often appended with the condition '…if it's not going to be great?'

Painting a landscape, writing a play, playing a piano concerto. Unless it's going to hang in the National Gallery, what's the point? Unless it's going to sell out Broadway, what's the point? Unless the Queen of England and half her court bear witness to the magnificence that is your piano-playing prowess, what's the point?

The problem with 'what the point?' is it makes us feel there has to be one before we can even start.

It thinks that the destination is the only thing that is important. It is not so much about the thing you create at the end of the process as the fun you had getting through it. The journey brings us fulfilment, learning, a sense of self. Often there is no clear and obvious 'point' to doing the creative thing we've chosen, and that's okay, right?

HONK! 'Wrong!' Okay, so some of you really need a point before you go any further. For your convenience, I've made a list. A nice long list bulleted for handiness.

It helps us connect with a quieter part of our brains;

It allows us forget about life for a while;

You get the chance to bring something new into the world, and that is particularly cool. Knitting a tea cosy. Baking brown bread. Writing a one-woman play. Telling a brand new joke.

Each new creation brings something to someone; purpose is what we humans are all about. In this way, the tea cosy allows us answer the phone and come back to a hot cuppa. The brown bread nourishes us. The play entertains, highlights, consoles. The joke makes our friend or neighbour or audience laugh;

Egos are great and all, but don't they make life that little bit crazier? Nothing slaps manners on an ego like creativity. Do yourself a favour: leave your conceits at the door;

Making newness gives flavour to the world, and there's always room for more of that;

Whether we create to help ourselves or others, creativity helps connect us to other people (most of the time this increases our sense of value and worth, but there's always an exception!);

Creativity lightens our lives when something HEAVY has fallen on us;

Doing something silly gives us head space;

Creating helps us appreciate all that we have;

It is better than a pill;

It is cheaper than therapy;

It is more effective than dieting;

It can't give you a hangover;

It's fun (and we all deserve a little fun).

You are welcome.

8 WE CAN'T ALL BE CREATIVE, CAN WE?

This question really matters to some people, maybe even to you, so let's address it head on: the idea that only certain people are creative. Maybe you believe you're one of the unlucky ones, that you haven't a creative bone in your body.

It's not an uncommon thought. Some people believe you're either born with creativity or you're not. They see creativity as something that cannot be taught.

They think that being creative is the same as being talented.

Here's what I think: I believe we are all creative. I believe that creativity comes in many forms. It shows itself in different ways. And while it's true that we are each born with potential, it's the doing something with that potential that brings about talent.

Potential needs to be given a chance, thrown a rope. It needs to be cared for and nurtured. It needs to be valued for what it is today, not for something it must become tomorrow.

Sometimes, potential is simply not spotted, other times not nurtured (and there are many reasons for this). Even when it is spotted and nurtured, it can sometimes be killed off by jealousy, anger, or impatience. When it comes down to it, potential on its own is dull and uninteresting. It is flawed and prone to mistakes.

Talent on the other hand is shiny and fascinating. Talent gets things right.

Talent is talked about, valued morally and intellectually, and often monetarily.

Talent is highly prized and sought after.

It is admired.

It is ooh'd and aah'd over.

Its origins are pondered over, its development a constant source of mystery. We look at the film actor and think 'what's his secret?' The recording artist is pulled apart like a lab specimen – 'how did she get to where she is?' We hold a magnifying glass to the poet, our wide eyes watchful for a glimpse of the magic behind his work.

In today's western civilisation, Talent is king while Creativity is the monarch's dresser, running around sourcing things to make Talent look good. Creativity in all its forms is widely undervalued. It is underused. It is too often misunderstood, ridiculed, or dismissed.

NOTES ON THIS CHAPTER:

A reminder that you'll find all the activities from this book in one handy *Safe Hands* workbook. Go to my website: www.nikkiweston.com/safe-hands-the-book and scroll down to find the free printable workbook in .doc or .pdf format.

Activity 1:

What do you think? Do you believe you are creative? Have you always felt this way?

____

____

____

Do you think your creative outlet would be valued and understood by others? By yourself?

____

____

____

How many creative forms can you think of? Push the boat out a bit. Think of some creative forms beyond the familiars like writing, art, and music.

____

____

____

9 YOUR TURN

You knew it would come, didn't you? Firstly, let me say something. You've made a big effort to be here, and I'm so glad to see you, but it's time we talked.

Who are you, really? And why are you here?

Was that too direct? Too scary? Okay, I'll tone it down and explain.

Maybe you're like me, spending years chasing something you knew was worthwhile, but ultimately followed a different kind of agenda. We all need a home, food on the table, and money. These are great goals, but there are others too.

Maybe you spent years being indifferent to your own needs.

Maybe something bugs you and the more you ignore it, the louder it gets. The self is very wise, it keeps knocking at our door until we answer.

Are you here because you're curious about pursuing something? Are you here because you're terrified about going back into something you did before? Are you here because you need support to take the first step?

Hands up if you're worried.

Hands up if you think this won't help you.

Hands up if your arm is aching from holding it up in the air this long.

Relax. You're not alone. We all feel scared about taking a step into the future, and sometimes we even feel scared of heading back into the known.

You're in good company, I'm right beside you and will hold your hand as you answer the next few questions and take your first steps. You'll realise that, whether you pursue your creative thing or you don't, the sky won't fall in.

Activity 2:

Way back when, who were you?

____

____

____

Where is that part of you?

____

____

____

What does it look like (is it in black and white, or colour; pattern or plain; vague or detailed)? Does it have a taste, a smell, a feel, a sound? Describe it here (or use the white space to draw it).

10 WHAT IS YOUR ACTIVITY?

What creative things did you do in the past that made you happy?

Think about the activities you used to enjoy before life got in the way.

It could be that you don't have the time, money, or energy for it anymore. Maybe you stopped liking it, and want to do something new. Either is cool.

I'll go first.

As a child, I used to knit. I loved embroidery and I was good at it. In my teens, I made clothes; I wasn't a great dressmaker, but I was good enough.

I used to sing. First, I sang in a school choir, then in my twenties I joined an amateur singing group, men and women. I did it out of curiosity, then it became a social outlet, and later, incredibly fulfilling. We met Monday nights. If you couldn't make it, it was fine. It wasn't school; there were no tests or teachers. It wasn't a job, there were no pay scales. You weren't fired if you failed to turn up once in a while, or if like me, you couldn't read music.

As a child, I dabbled in calligraphy, getting a gorgeous little beginner's set from my brother. I dabbled in it and absolutely loved it until exams and university and life came calling. Then a few years ago, when thriller writer Brenda Novak and I connected, she needed something cool to auction at her Diabetes fundraiser, 'For the Cure'. I remembered my love for inking and lettering, and I thought 'why the hell not'. I bought myself a slightly better calligraphy set, a watercolour pad, and created a dozen or so pieces that I sent to Brenda's offices in California, raising a cool $700 for her very valuable cause. Not bad for a lassie who thought she couldn't draw.

I did rock-climbing. I do not want to do it again.

It's cool to remember these things and why I did them. It's also important to remember that I wasn't always 'qualified' or experienced in them. I practised calligraphy on my own, with a book or two and a lot of mistakes, but I did it and people bought my pieces.

Think of your past pursuits. Remember that you're not contracted to do any of these things again. For now, just recall them and gently consider whether or not you might want to do them again.

11 PASSION

Passion is the fire inside you that won't go out, the daydream that creeps into your Monday and gets you thinking about something other than the here and now. I always think that if the here and now we had was the here and now that we wanted, we'd be better able to stay in the moment a bit more. What I want is not in this moment, not entirely. I have a drive to write and share my thoughts, to help others, to touch lives and effect change however small.

I'm good with people. That is, I like connecting with people and I'm good at it. I've been told it too, which is reassuring. But even when we're told something, we don't always believe it. To effect change, we have to believe the thing ourselves.

Like I do. I believe that I would nail some Japanese drumming. Other times, I yearn to free my inner Debbie Harry and bring a Blondie tribute band to Dublin disco. I frequently tell myself I am epic at mixing colours, then I wonder why everything on my canvas resembles pea-green soup. I even fantasise about barking out navigation instructions to a revved-up rally driver; in my head, we'd shred that chequered flag (if only I could tell left from right).

And now and then, I even believe I can write.

Writing has always been my medium of choice. I write fiction and non-fiction and try to sell it. I dream up new stuff all the time. I make decent calligraphy for charity, I make collages for my mental health, and I make terrible art for a large envelope on my bookshelf. But you know what, I'm doing the things I love.

Writing is my passion. It is words and drive and ideas that come to me at the most inconvenient of times. It races relentlessly toward me every day with the same anger and roar, demanding to be heard, heeded, fed. When I ignore it, it persists. It gets angry, and rightly so. I said I would look after it, and when I stop, when some other part of life needs me and I can't feed the beast right away, it gets angrier.

When you feed it, passion gets quiet. It stops bothering you til tomorrow. It allows you to get back to the kids or the dog or your friends. It allows you catch some z's. Then it wakes you and starts all over again.

That's passion.

Activity 3:

Just for fun, list one or two things you might like to try, say, in the short or medium-term future.

____

____

____

12 ROLES

All the world's a stage, they say, and everyone has their roles to play. But what happens when you have too many? On the next page, see Activity 4.

Activity 4: Which of these apply to you?

Daughter	Son	Sister	Brother	Mother	Father
Wife	Husband	Partner	Lover	Volunteer	Shit-stirrer
Boyfriend	Grandparent	Neighbour	Fighter	Counsellor	Activist
Girlfriend	Great grandparent	Friend	Cleaner-upper	Peacemaker	Fortune teller
Financer	Busybody	Facilitator	Doormat	Photographer	Snitch
Spy	Confidante	Envier	Knitter	Musician	Sceptic
Objective thinker	Devil's advocate	Historian	Drama queen/king	Essayist	Glory Hunter
Mentor	Stalker	Carer	Listener	Poet	Saint
Playwright	Inventor	Stylist	Talker	Gardener	Warm-up act
Leader	Event planner	Shopper	Voice of reason	Painter	Show-stopper
Carer	Caretaker	Entrepreneur	Victim	Director	Gossip
Politician	Comedian	Diplomat	Empath	Songwriter	Prosecutor
Pleaser	Waster	Mess-clearer	Dreamer	Illustrator	Seamstress
Sponger	Riddler	Designer	Sidekick	Addict	Student
Fighter	Catastrophist	Crutch	Joker	Gatekeeper	Dancer
Interrogator	Composer	Zealot	Fixer	Actor	Follower
Memoirist	Sheep	Screenwriter	Criminal	Writer	Teacher
Artist	Navigator	Hero	Spendthrift	Miser	Narcissist
Dogwalker	Dogsbody	Ruler	Rule-maker	Deputy	Shadow

13 ESSENTIALS AND EXTRAS

We all have essential roles (husband, sister, friend), and then there are the extras. Think of an extra like something we do almost by accident: lightening the tone with a joke can make us a comedian, a diplomat, or an empath; giving in to the petty demands of a moody boss can mean we are pleasers, peace-keepers, or that we simply remain in employment.

Some extra roles are a little more eye-catching. They include things like confidante, hero, or glory hunter. They shine and bling. We often regard them as cool or important. We catch ourselves looking longingly at them, admiring our bravery or capability or both. An extra role can masquerade as something noble ('Your two long-time friends are warring with each other? Why not be the Mediator!'), but do it enough times and you find you've become a Doormat.

Extra roles can be hard work, so let's call them Exhausting Extras. Exhausting Extras are roles that leave us feeling drained or unhappy, confused or depressed, resentful, or angry. An Exhausting Extra drains your energy and leaves you high and dry.

It's all very well to suggest we choose it, as if we can get out of it, or like we don't really have to do it in the first place. But it's hard to argue that it's a waste of our time. Isn't there always some justification for an exhausting extra, some cause that is worth supporting?

We tell ourselves that we really should be the event planner for a big family get-together so that bickering siblings don't escalate to full-on fisticuffs. We tell ourselves we don't mind offering a lift to our nosey patronising friend even if it means we'll have to endure a half-hour's inquisition about our badly paid job. And wouldn't it be a good thing to finalise your overdue thesis tomorrow, using today to support your hot new boyfriend as he leads an all-day rally against a company you've never even heard of?

Notice the seduction, the need we feel to say yes. It pulls us closer, making us think that this about being there for other people. But it rarely makes our lives better. Most of the time it's nothing more than a hurdle thrown in front of us to slow us down, or worse, stop us.

Sometimes an Exhausting Extra appears to be useful or entertaining, a way to pass the time, a coping mechanism for everyday life. Your job would be boring if it weren't for the daily gossip session with Doris in Reception. And if you didn't dis your kid's schoolteachers, what in the name of all that is holy would you and the school gate moms talk about?

What if (brace yourself Bridie) we swap one coping mechanism for another? One that is not exhausting? One that's maybe a teensy bit enjoyable? One that helps ease the pain, not add to it?

14 EXTRA! EXTRA! READ ALL ABOUT IT!

Like a newspaper boy calling out a headline, Extras sound sensational. They're exciting. They reel us in. They're often dramatic, they can be seductive, and they're oh-so-addictive. But what is worst is that Extras are roles we allow ourselves into. We choose them.

Sure, we feel pulled in that direction, either by other people or circumstances. Who hears the APB that Exhausting Extras send out, only to stick their hands up and says they'll take it on?

No one forces us, do they? There's no gun to our head.

Whether it is done consciously or not, we allow ourselves slide into being the gossip, the busybody, or the judge. The financier, the sceptic, the leader.

It's ourselves who walk up and take it, and it's ourselves who allow us to stay. Why?

Because it's easy. We've been doing that thing for so long, we've become Successful. We've been being that person for so long that we've come to enjoy it a hell of a lot more than trying something new.

'Something new' might fail. In fact, there's a damn good chance that it will fail.

Isn't it easier to stick with what we know? Spreading gossip about someone, whether true or not, is far more satisfying than picking up a pen and writing. Spending time deliberating the guilt or innocence of a friend's marital infidelity is much more fun than practising that piano piece whose second section keeps frustrating the heck out of us.

Imagining worst-case scenarios of starting that business or painting that flower pot or writing that poem distracts us enough to make sure we never actually apply for our trading licence or root out the paint pots or jot down that first line. Distraction is fabulous, and it's fun.

Activity 5: Role-play!

1. Think about your roles. Which ones are Essential?

____

____

____

2. Identify some of the Exhausting Extras (EEs) that affect you. The ones that leave you feeling low or angry are particularly good. Jot them down:

____

____

____

3. Finish this: if this EE wasn't in my life, I would feel…

____

____

____

4. Finish this: if this EE wasn't taking up my time, I might have time to…

____

____

____

PART TWO: FEELING

'Every sun casts a shadow...'
    TAKEN FROM BOOK 'THE WAR OF ART'
    BY STEVEN PRESSFIELD

15 DANGER! DANGER! HIGH VOLTAGE!

Remember that Exhausting Extra you mentioned? How would you feel if I told you the next part of Safe Hands is to drop that role? How would you react if I told you you don't have a choice? That I'm going to force you, right now, to stop being a judge or a drama queen or a dogsbody?

Stop right there. I don't know about you, but I don't react well to requests like these. If someone asks me to stop doing something that has been my crutch for not trying other harder stuff, I stand there and pretend to listen. I am secretly seething, but politeness forces me to stay put.

Even if they're nicey-nice about it, giving a helpful tip or advice to make your life better, it matters not a jot. It doesn't change how I feel; I'm still furious. The rug's been pulled out from under me. My defences flare and my blood quickens, all while smiling politely and fighting the urge to tell them 'no' ninja-style.

Forcing someone to do something is both disingenuous and

foolhardy. Like when your spouse tries to get you to quit smoking. We say we'll do it, if only to shut them up, then spend the rest of the week resenting them and suggesting they go out with their friends just long enough for you to steal a sneaky smoke out the window as soon as they've left.

We know that if we drop our EE, we'll have to face other stuff. Stuff we want to ignore or forget. The legal paperwork over your mother's estate. The disagreement with your kid's father. The fear that keeps you puffing on a cigarette while you staunchly ignore the truth ('so maybe these things are killing me').

We use that extra role to keep ourselves warm and dry. It's our insta-reason, our go-to justification that's forever ready should some helpful busybody suggest that we could and should hire a specialist lawyer, arrange to cross town and negotiate with the ex on their turf, see if the doctor can refer to you a stop smoking clinic (and treat that hacking cough that's keeping you awake).

Exhausting extras are not excuses, oh no! We have answers to the barrage of questions that you'll proceed to challenge us with. Explanations, statistics, studies, or anecdotes that support our reason. This isn't the first time we've been pushed off the lounger into the water. We've tested it before, and this baby is watertight. We've made sure that our extra role is viable and sensible and rock-solid. How dare they try and throw me in headfirst, you think, as you grip the armrests good and tight.

When an exhausting extra is so addictive, and the withdrawal so risky, can we ever give it up?

Yes, if we approach the enemy slowly and safely.

When it looked like I was 'forcing' you to give up your role, what did you feel? If you felt relief or joy, then my market research is all wrong, and you do not need to read MY book ;-)

If you didn't, read on.

16 GETTING TO KNOW YOU

When I feel pressure to change, it can only mean one thing: fear. Anne, a friend of mine, once said to me that fear isn't that different from excitement. 'No way,' I told myself, 'excitement is fun and generally means something good is about to happen'.

But on second thought, isn't that exactly what fear does?

Your stomach tightens. Your mind kicks off, anticipating good, bad, and ugly. It's true that with fear, you fret and moan you and try and get out of it, but when you act in the face of fear, very often the good thing that you hoped would happen, happens.

That presentation you were terrified about goes better than you thought; suddenly, you've got yourself a new client;

The elaborate marriage proposal plan atop Sydney Harbour Bridge doesn't quite roll according to plan (to Alan, with apologies); but she accepts anyway and, years from now, the story will regale your kids;

As you wait in the theatre wings, the impatient clatter of a preview audience makes your mouth go dry — but the next day, the reviews are favourable.

So yeah, Anne knows what she's talking about.

Fear prepares us in so many ways. It gets us ready even though our hearts and heads feel like we never will be. I've tried ignoring it (fools no one), staring it down (causes paralysis), harnessing it as a motivator (seriously?)…

I accept that I have to deal with fear, but I do it on my terms. So here is a tool I have used time and again. It's not sophisticated or technical, but since no one's here to stop me, I am going to claim it in the name of Ireland: the delicious habit Irish people have of poking fun at something. We do it for lots of reasons, but it's generally to slow, to weaken, or disarm a problem.

'Taking the Mick', as we call it, is the Irish way of joking about something in order to calm everything down before the issue gets too serious. Known elsewhere as ribbing, razzing, ragging, teasing, pulling someone's chain; wherever you're from, you know what I mean.

Making fun of fear can take the sting out of it, changing its shape and form long enough for us to see it as another part of our daily landscape, a feature of every journey, a sign that says up ahead is something good.

NOTES ON THIS CHAPTER:

'Taking the Mick' has been officially credited with saving a daily average of 10,083 Irish friendships and half as many marriages. The latter figures are due to the assumption that the intimate nature of marriage can potentially increase offence levels; if there is a risk of this in your marriage, we advise that you 'Take the Mick' only if spouse's friends and family are firmly out of earshot. Data supplied by Irish Society for the Prevention of Serious Shit.

Activity 6: Flip the F.E.A.R

Using the letters F, E, A, and R as an acronym, write three sentences that are not scary. For example: 'Fierce edam and ricotta'; 'Fracture each amazing racket'; 'Fluting elephants are real'.

No limits, no rules, no right, no wrong. Just play. Tune in to the feeling of playing with something.

Revel in the letters and what they might stand for. Let the words come out in whatever form they choose.

Give it a try:

1. ____

2. ____

3. ____

How does it feel? Have you managed to put a little distance between fear and you?

Notice the fun in this F.E.A.R activity. Snuggle up to the lines you came up with. Feel the ridiculousness.

Shining a nonsensical light onto fear (or anything) relieves the dark times. This humble exercise is useful for anything that 'puts the heart crossways' in us. Use it next time you are facing something difficult.

17 RESISTANCE

In his book, 'The War of Art', Steven Pressfield takes fear and gives it a more appropriate name of Resistance, complete with a capital R. Resistance is a force, he says, and his book gives shape and form to an enemy that imposes on us from the outside as well as from within.

Pressfield talks about an opponent that tries to stop us from bettering ourselves and our world. Resistance is anything that keeps you from taking a step forward, in creativity or anything else for that matter.

Resistance is a bit like fear, but it's bigger again. It is a force, whether you believe it to be real or not. Resistance is anything that tries to stop change. Can you imagine that?

Resistance believes that pursuing creativity should not be done. It is the voice that says you have too many responsibilities to strum a guitar while the dinner's cooking. It is the phone call that comes when you sit down to draft a short story. It is the printer that fails to cooperate when you've a rake of paper-and-red-pen edits to do...

The problem is when we let Resistance in. When we decide that tonight, rather than pick guitar strings to 'Castle on the Hill', we will not only mash the potatoes, but we'll puree them too, making a big old mess that we'll have to spend ages cleaning up. Or when we see our PTA Chair's number and take the call anyway. When we give up on trying to fix the printer, the edits, or anything really, and instead turn on Facebook.

Understanding Resistance has changed my life (oh no, there's those three little words).

Hear me out: understanding what Resistance is has stopped me blaming myself for my creative stops and starts. Knowledge is power, and once I understood resistance, I was able to recognise it.

According to Pressfield, Resistance is:
invisible;
internal;
insidious (it is always lying and is always full of shit);
implacable (it cannot be reasoned with, it never tires or stops);
impersonal (it's not out to get you personally, it just 'is')
infallible;
universal;
It never sleeps;
It plays for keeps;
It is fuelled by fear;
It only opposes in one direction (up!);
It is most powerful at the finish line;

It recruits allies (saboteurs, including ourselves).

If you hear nothing else in this book, hear this: Resistance "is fear, it lives inside all of us, and it attacks us when we try to do anything that rejects immediate gratification in favour of long-term growth, health, or integrity. Or, expressed another way, any act that derives from our higher nature instead of our lower one."

In other words, instead of choosing to believe that a failed audition was your fault – that you're just a crap actor and should give up now – it is in fact down to Resistance. So if I have failed at something, it isn't my inabilities or laziness or crapness that's to blame. In fact, it's got nothing to do with what I am or am not. If it was, then I would have to quit, right?

Resistance is something outside of me. I can see that this isn't a personal failure. Once I know this, and can recognize Resistance when it occurs, I can do something about it and crucially, I can keep going.

Learning about Resistance told me that my rejected manuscripts were not a sign that I was crap and should quit. It was a sign that I had to keep going, keep working and thinking of ways around the problem.

Knowing that there's a force opposing me and everything I'm working for is a revelation! So it's NOT me who's crap or lazy or thick or lazy or crap. There's something else at play here, and I can do something about it.

64

18 HORSE MANURE AND B.S.

Bookshelves the world over claim that we can be fearless, quash our nerves, conquer our procrastination and paralysis and live a fear-free life. And boy does that byline sell books. It's the Holy Grail; the promise of blue skies and endless possibilities.

HONK! I call BS.

As a goal one should strive toward, 'fearless' is idealistic and unhelpful. As a concept, it is false.

No matter what we do, we can't erase it inside of ourselves. Nor can we create a world without it. Fear exists. It has its functions and its reasons for being. Let me repeat this: Fear exists. I've seen it, and felt it, and I have to say I respect that creature. When I don't, it gets the better of me. When I don't, it gets its claws into me, and before I know it, I'm crying on the floor roaring 'I can't'.

Ah, the things we tell ourselves.

Resistance hates when we try. It hates harder when we try a second time. When we test our tenacity, our desire, our nerve to try a third time, it gets angry and shows its true colours. It will never stop trying to stop us from improving our lot in life. Obstacle after obstacle shows up. Piles of crap all over the place.

I'm suggesting we make peace with fear, for a short while at least. It's not letting it win, fear will never leave us, and it's pointless trying to force it. It's a force in itself, so how about picking it up and using it for your own gain? For what matters to you?

19 TAP-TAP-TAP

I call writing my need-to-do. It's the first whisper to my waking brain: it bounces along the synapses, reminding me of what it wants me to do. But I ignore it: I've got my own plan for the day. "I don't have time, my boss is giving me hell, and and and…"

An hour later, I feel a tap on the shoulder. My need-to-do is there, niggling, pestering, nagging. I keep tending to whatever I was doing, and raise my voice. "I told you already: I don't have time, the youngest is sick, my boss is giving me hell, my dog needs the vet and that's one more bill I can't afford, and and and…"

I'm the gatekeeper, or so I tell myself; we are following my rules.

I'm busy meeting a customer or a doctor or a friend, raising a family, bringing the car to the shop, and then I feel a push and I stumble. My need-to-do has gotten bigger since I looked at it, stronger. It challenges me, but I answer back. "I've gotten more since the last time," I tell it, "and no they aren't excuses, they are reasons, I am a real person, with real problems… and and and…"

But my need-to-do doesn't move. It stays right there. It calls long and loud into my ear, until I stick my fingers in my ears and start singing 'Can you tell me how to get to Sesame Street?'

My need-to-do is drowning, and that's alright with me. 'Job done,' I think to myself, 'I showed that writing who's boss; it's only a thing I do now and then anyway, isn't it? Besides, I've other fish to fry, important fish, so writing will just have to wait.'

But after a while, things get hard. Paying attention to everything and everyone else has me out of sorts. There's something wrong, I just can't quite put my finger on it. Then something big happens— the old car dies and we've to find money from nowhere, someone close is suddenly ill—and I move into cope mode. I try holding it all together this way then that, but I can't, I don't. I am so worn out and vulnerable that I bawl and cry and completely fall apart.

Pause.

Familiar anyone? Do you too feel that you should be able to go happily along ignoring the taps and the nagging? Do you too take your eyes off the Crazy dial and next time you look find that everything's at 10? Do you too fall apart?

I'm sorry. It's the pits, no?

What's really the pits is the fact that my need-to-do doesn't care about life. Let me be clear: my need-to-do is programmed to stand there all the live-long day and nag me until I turn around and let it out. Until I park my reasons and my life, and do just a little. Something. Anything to ease the tension and anger. Collage for 10 minutes. Scribble with a pen for 5. Breathe for 1.

Only I don't. I have the fear, and that mo-fo is on my side and it is nothing short of tenacious. It works for me, it puts stuff on hold so that I can be and do all the roles that life expects me to be. Fear protects me, stopping me from growing or changing even a little bit. After a while, my life gets bananas. I can't think straight. There's not enough time or money or energy for anything anymore, and I can't cope with the kids or the parents or the bills or the crazy. So I scream, so loud and long that after a while I can't hear whispers of any sort.

I've gotten my way alright, yessir! I stayed in control (mostly). So why do I feel so crap?

That's when it dawns on me: I have not gotten my way. Not an inch. Nothing's changed, nothing's got better. The Crazy dial is at its max, and I realise it's been hammering at 10. All. This. Time.

The only thing that's got its way is Fear.

On the other hand, my whisper is long gone.

20 WHISPERING AND ROARING

You've heard them, right? The words whispered into your ear. Your need-to-do talks to you when you least expect it: in the early morning; stopped in traffic, staring at nothing.

The whisper of possibility is when something or someone says you'd be good at something, a suggestion of something you'd enjoy. The memory of a past creative pursuit you dabbled in and dropped.

Whispers come to me in the shower when there's suds in my eyes and I'm running late and I haven't a shred of paper to record the idea: a scene in a play I didn't think I needed to write; a line that would sound amazing being spoken by a hero I've not yet met; an idea for a book or a workshop that would interest others as well as myself.

I risk freezing wet floor tiles and pad out to the bedroom for a pen. Whispers are slight and hard to hear, but they sound a bit like this:

What's the worst that can happen?

Indeed, the worst that can happen is that we don't heed it.

It's not our fault; there's something competing for our attention. The roar of failure. It's that voice long and loud that snaps the possibility right out of you. It tells you all the ways you'd be rubbish at something, and it has gazillions of them.

The roar of failure sounds like this:

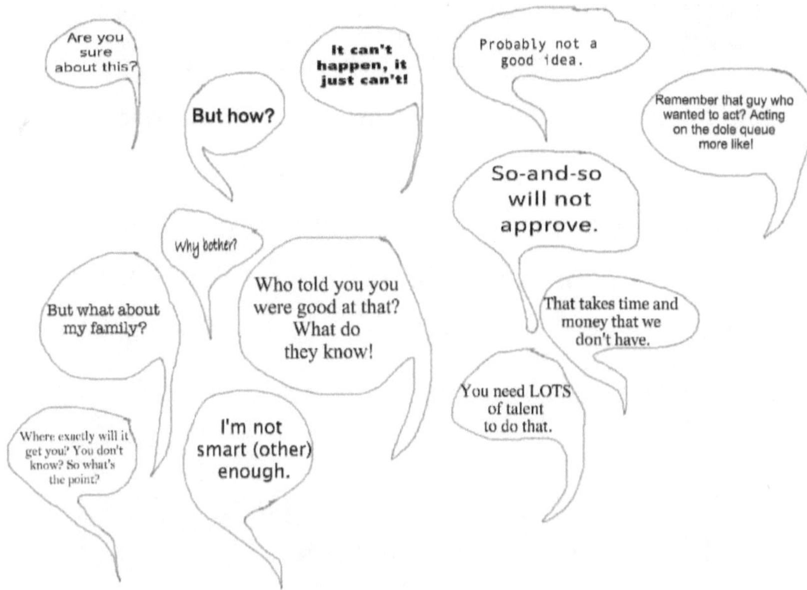

The roar proves that the squeaky wheel really does get the most oil. We pay attention to it, not only out of self-preservation but also because some of these are really hard to argue with. When there's even a little bit of truth there, we'd do well to sit up and listen, right?

I mean, yeah, so-and-so did try doing something like what I want to do and it didn't work out. I've never written a song before so I guess you're right, I don't know how to do it. Sure, writing and putting on my own play is kinda pie-in-the-sky. It's hard. It can fail. I can fail, and I guess there's a big chance that I will fail—

Wait, did I just say that? Aren't I supposed to be helping you? So why the negative talk? In all honesty, I talk like this to myself all the time, and have done most of my life. The roar of failure gains traction when we are young, and builds rapidly. It's loud, it's authoritative, and it tells everyone exactly what it thinks of them.

It sounds as if it really knows its shit. The trouble starts when I believe it knows its shit, and boy do I.

Part of the problem is that the roar of failure has a protective ring. It talks logically. It sounds correct. It sounds like it's only looking out for me. This is the hard part. This is the part I wish didn't exist. This is the part that I don't have easy answers for. It's the time when others might tell me to push through. Decide how much I want it. 'You have a choice', they might tell me, 'go big or go home'. Or 'You have NO choice, so you may as well just feel the fear and do it anyway.'

(Shudder)

The problem with feeling the fear and doing it anyway is that it's paralysing.

The roar comes dangerously close to what we want for ourselves: the quiet life, the path of least resistance, no muss no fuss.

The roar seems to presume that when we say we want to act, that we are shooting for a six-figure paycheque and an Oscar to boot. When I said 'I'd love to write a song', the roar took it to mean 'I'd love to write a song that goes platinum in 37 countries'.

The roar is a thing of extremes. It snipes and fights and stands firmly by its guns. There's no negotiating with the roaring. There's no cajoling so it might see our point of view. It's too busy talking its own propaganda to hear anything you have to say. Nothing and no one will change its mind; arguing only perpetuates the struggle. So do yourself a favour and save your breath. Try another way.

21 SMALL HANDS

The roaring is a little bit like a child who reacts to something that's been done to them. If he feels he's been treated harshly, the child lashes out, arms and legs flung around the place. His language is strong, his face is tense. He's angry and he's loud and he's right in front of us, waving his hands.

Gently, slowly, take one of those hands in yours.

Look closely. Feel its weight and size; it is smaller than we thought. Notice the soft skin, the gentle lines on the palm, the fingertips rounded just like ours. The hand may be trembling. It may be clammy or tense.

What to do?

We're not going to roar back at it, or throw proof of our rightness in their face. It's not about shutting anyone up, proving anything wrong.

The roar wants to protect us. It's scared for us. Scared for what we are about to do. It's frightened because it too has been pummelled and trodden on. Forgotten and ignored. This child's heart is frightened, terrified, and desperate to protect itself. It is not doubting our abilities. It values us. It values our dreams. It values our abilities.

It is simply afraid for what we are about to go through.

22 HELPING HANDS

I guess that, at my centre, I'm still a child. I feel fear like a kid does, knowing there's something under the bed, the same something that disappears as soon as a light goes on. I often need help starting things, and sometimes, I need a minute or two to be sure I can do something.

I need small. I need gentle.

Thinking this way isn't right or wrong; but when it comes to fear and taking one small step, it is helpful for me. It is not guaranteed to always work, but it helps. It's my life I'm leading, my hands doing the doing, my dreams realised or not, and I could do with all the help I can get.

The roar of failure is not quiet, but I've acknowledged his worry and held his hand. But like a schoolchild who needs to play her own game, I know it's time to let him go. I take a tiny step in a direction that's all my own. Bringing my energy bit by bit from worry, and pain, and fear, toward something altogether more deserving, more productive. Myself. My hands. My life.

I have time and space to let me start the thing I'm wanting to do. Taking the evening class in acrylics. Buying the ukelele. Snapping wildlife with my camera phone.

And later, when the bell goes for hometime, I realise I've been lost in this activity for minutes, hours, and I've enjoyed every second. I grab my schoolbag and coat, and look around. My old friend fear is still over there but he's okay. He's found other people to hang out with, and the sky is still holding up.

23 TRUSTING HANDS

To keep going, we need support. Reassurance that we have succeeded at other things:

- My cakes have turned out well nearly every time, so there's a likelihood I'll pull off this Wedding Cake for my son.

- I was so nervous before my driver's test but I held it together and passed, so there's a chance I can get through this audition.

- A handful of folks have liked my fiction ideas before, so this acquiring editor just might buy the anthology I'm pitching.

Mining our past successes for nuggets of proof backs up Failure's never-ending demands for evidence that we might have a clue what we are doing. In time, it helps us build trust in ourselves. In an ideal world, belief in our abilities would come mostly from us, but often it comes from other people.

One of my first paid writing jobs was for a book distribution company.

Years before either of us had kids, a friend of mine had kindly read my early fiction, a short novella about a young American woman studying voice and opera in Madrid. It wasn't very good, but at the time, Katie had given me useful feedback, and was kind and encouraging.

Back to the present, and Katie dropped me an email. The book company she worked for needed a 900-1000 word article around the realities of parenting, promoting parenting books that I might be able to recommend. There was a decent rate of pay and she wondered would I be interested?

Hell yeah! I'd read every parenting book going! Although I still didn't know how to parent, I could give others a steer; maybe with their heads in a book, their kids wouldn't bother them (Ha! If only!)

So I sat down and vomited out 400 rough words. Like they were really rough. I was so disgusted with them/myself that I left it for a week or two, distracting myself and panicking over my procrastination. Our annual extended-family vacation on Ireland's West Coast island of Achill was only days away, so I busied myself with buying supplies, planning what is always a busy holiday week. I'm not into spas or sports, but I felt a sudden urge to learn all about Achill's rich tourism industry of seaweed baths and surf schools and ignore finishing the article.

Backstory: I admire and respect Katie; she is one of life's absolute gems. Witty and modest, among many other things she is an accomplished writer and editor. At the time she was a new mother, so I really did not want to complicate her life or waste her time. Plus, the book company was way cooler and more exciting than me; their articles used a higher register with language that sounded proper literary, like.

Holy crap.

Okay, so I write casual (can't you tell?); the last paid writing job I'd had was for a dating website and that was years before. It's embarrassing to think of the days and nights I'd spent writing articles like 'Dating pitfalls in the Workplace', only to earn The Smallest Paycheque Ever.

So I rattled round the house, telling myself I couldn't do it; I hadn't trained as an articles writer; the kids were still so small, I was up to my eyes and there just wasn't time…

I waited three weeks, then emailed with words along the lines of 'Thanks Katie, but I don't think I'm the right person for the job…', 'only 400 words…', 'it's rougher than a badger's backside…'

I was sure she'd say 'ah that's okay Nic, no worries. I'll get someone else'.

Okay, so I HOPED she'd say that. Isn't that why I waited three flaming weeks to get back to her? If she couldn't get an article to bring back to HQ, she would simply have to find someone else and little old me would be off the hook! Hooray!

But she replied. She really wanted to see what I could do.

I was confused: hadn't she read my plotless lesbian erotica? Critiqued the ménage-a-trois scene I'd rewritten a million times? Waded through emotions I had killed by overwriting, and—the pièce de résistance—my horrendous Spanish lyrics to a fictional aria my bisexual Maria-Callas protagonist belts out at the, um, 'height of her performance'?

I will never forget Katie's email: the rush of reassurance about my casual writing style, her invitation to take my time, her kind offer to read an early draft and give me a steer. Her gentle confidence that whatever I would submit couldn't possibly be as bad as some things she'd read (she'd obviously forgotten my song lyrics from 'El Sueño'…).

Somehow Katie believed in me.

(I'm glad one of us did.)

In her email, I found more than just time and reassurance; I felt permitted to make mistakes; I felt protected. She told me not to worry, that she would let me know if it wasn't right, and that (only if I wanted to) I should give it another try.

So I agreed, with a small get-out clause: if Katie didn't receive the article before I had to leave for Achill on Saturday morning, she could assume it wasn't coming. The calendar showed 5 days, so I pulled out the 400 words. They weren't total crap. In fact, some of it was good. Bits were funny. Bits gave me ideas for more words.

As I wrote for Katie, the thrill of the job, the enjoyment of the doing, flooded me. And I remembered that I'd felt like this before: writing the dating articles had taken a total of 45 hours over two weeks (I know…). It paid the princely sum of $90 (heaven help us, I know!!!). It made me fret and doubt myself but, of the writing at least, I enjoyed every single minute.

I busted a gut to get Katie's article done and half-ways healthy by Friday morning. That night I proofread it and, Saturday morning, did a (dozen more) 'final' reads. I'd barely hit 'Send' when an editor emailed me back to say thanks and she'd be in touch.

I felt nauseous but it could have been the diesel fumes while my husband waited in the car to drive all of us the four hours from Dublin to Achill Island. August was indeed a wicked month: the rain in Mayo seemed to come down in rivers, so we were largely confined to a crazy crowded house on the Wild Atlantic Way: just me, my husband, our kids, my parents, my siblings, their spouses, their kids…

Between the seaweed, surf, and squabbles, I checked my inbox so I could sooner read Katie's flat refusal to use the article, get over the news that she hated me, my fiction, and now my non-fiction, and that she'd added me to her list of never-hire-again writers. At least then I could justify downing a litre or two of Bailey's Irish cream and perhaps enjoy what was left of the world's wettest holiday.

Tuesday morning and Achill's Atlantic rain lashed off the double-glazing as I spotted an email from the editor. The article was great, she told me. She'd barely had to change a thing, and could I give her my PayPal details?

Instead of celebrating, I realised two things:

1 - I'd gone and done it. I'd sold my work for a decent price. Finally, it was published for all the world to see. 'Published' as in 'online', 'not coming off', 'ever'.

I considered hyperventilating but:

2 - my kids were wrestling their cousin on the wooden staircase outside and the clatter they were making said it was a matter of

seconds before one of them would need to be airlifted to a children's hospital for a spot of orthopaedic surgery.

Before I roared at the WWE wannabes, I clicked on the article link. I searched for the fixes, for the changes I was certain they'd had to make: semi-colon in the wrong place, a horrendous social faux pas, even a typo.

But it was unchanged. All 983 words were exactly as I had sent. It was good and they'd liked it, just as it was.

It taught me that even though I make mistakes, the world keeps turning, and I am allowed try again and again and again. And often I get it right.

How very reassuring.

Whenever you do your thing, be sure to look for a sign afterward. What do you notice?

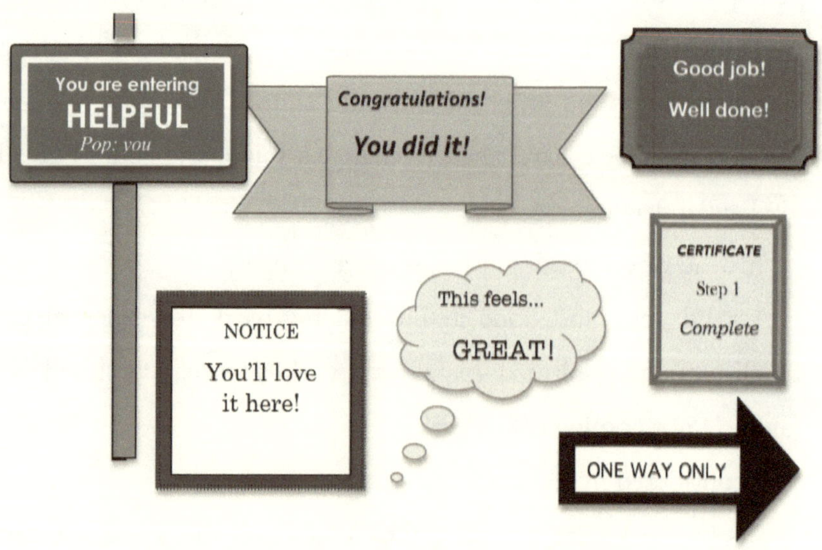

Activity 6 – Case of evidence

1. Write down 3 things that you did in the past that turned out well, either years ago, or yesterday - things that looked like they hadn't much chance of working out, but which succeeded as a direct result of your skills, persistence, and hard work. It can be big or it can be small.

____

____

____

2. Think of one of these successes. Think about the decisions you made in the face of problems, even the small ones. Think about the actions you took.

Write down the evidence of your success.

____

____

____

This is your own trust in yourself. Treat it well.

Congratulate yourself. Be grateful to yourself for all you did to bring the situation to the result you wanted.

3. Who were the people whose voices or actions helped you along?

____

4. Who in your life today trusts and believes in you?

24 PERMISSION

By and large, I don't allow myself much. There are tons of fun things like painting a still life or singing, things that the cold light of logic tells me will help me manage the other areas of my life.

But most of us don't work on logic, at least not all the time. Instead, I am caught up in the small matter of everyday life. Keeping plates upright and spinning is about as much as I can manage. Stepping away from that feels like clocking off. It feels like abandoning my responsibilities or downing tools for a while, and I've never been able to call it a day without first saying at least a 'So long' to the boss.

I want permission, but from who?

A boss? A spouse? God?

Permission comes only from myself. Just as I choose to deny myself one thing, I permit myself another.

Activity 7:

1. Do you need permission to take the first step?

____

____

____

2. If you feel you're needing permission from someone in your life, who is it? Are they likely to grant it and therefore be a help to you? If not them, who?

____

____

____

3. What small thing could you do today to grant permission to yourself?

____

____

____

4. To keep this sense of permission, what could you do tomorrow?

____

____

____

25 EPIC FAIL

In 2001, Tommy Wiseau wrote a movie, a romantic drama feature film that he called 'The Room'. An aspiring actor, Tommy had moved with his actor friend Greg Sestero to Los Angeles where getting a showbiz break seemed impossible. But Tommy was driven to succeed: one day he would make a movie of his own. Inspired by Brando, Dean, and other Hollywood stars, it would be inspiring, unforgettable, epic.

After months of writing a screenplay, he hired a film crew. Tommy was producer, director, lead actor, as well as being in charge of casting other actors including his friend Greg. He also financed the entire project himself, buying expensive equipment and weeks and weeks of studio time.

Filming is never easy, but Tommy got considerable criticism from the get go. Concerns about plot holes, bad dialogue, love scenes that bordered on ridiculous. Greg and others who cared deeply about their careers and about Tommy were helpless as he poured more money into a project that was clearly sad and pathetic.

Their worries fell on the deafest of ears. 'You have to believe', Tommy told them, and simply carried on regardless. His bad decisions and obstinacy drove everyone crazy.

Even when the money dried up, the schedule ran over again, and crew members stormed off in exasperation, Tommy insisted 'The Room' was going to be huge. He raised more money for editing and promotion, and finally, after 2 years and US$6 million, his movie was finished.

'The Room' had its world premiere in Los Angeles in June 2003. A proud Tommy arrived by limo and greeted his audience, promising them they would never forget this incredible movie. He took his seat beside Greg in the front row, and the lights went down.

A few minutes into the screening, the audience was stunned.

The movie wasn't bad—it was really bad…

From the start, 'The Room' was dying. The script was melodramatic drivel, and the actors delivering it were visibly uncomfortable. The plot had holes throughout, lacking logic, fluidity, or any level of common sense; subplots seemed to pop up at will and exit just as quickly. Scene continuity was a joke and the love scenes were hilarious.

Soon there was a snort. Then someone laughed. It wasn't long before the effect spread and the whole theatre—including Greg— was in hysterics. Clutching-of-sides, peeing-in-pants. The Room was the funniest craziest godawful movie they'd ever seen.

Tommy got to his feet and demanded they stop laughing.

Believing that this too was part of the show, they only laughed more. Ashamed and humiliated, he walked out.

In the foyer, he could hear his friends laughing, people he looked up to. People he was trying to impress. Tommy felt gutted. How could he have been so stupid, so blind? He'd ignored his friends advice, fought his critics, persisted ad nauseum. Hadn't he done everything he thought he needed to create a successful movie? Hadn't he followed his heart, worked tirelessly, against all the odds, only to release the summer's biggest disaster?

Greg followed him out. He begged his friend to reframe the project they had dreamed of for so long, a storyline that Tommy wanted to be epic. As gently as he could, Greg told Tommy that his creation, his movie, was indeed epic, just not in the way he'd wanted. He'd followed his dream, he'd pushed hard despite all the odds, and it was not a waste. 'Listen to them,' he told Tommy, 'they're enjoying it, aren't they?'

With a little help from his friends, Tommy managed to find value and worth in this disaster of a movie. He forgave himself enough to promote 'The Room', and while he never made his money back, his movie has a considerable cult following. It is celebrated as one of the best bad movies ever made, so much so that actor brothers James and Dave Franco made 'The Disaster Artist', a 2017 film about the making of The Room, an unforgettable movie that is truly epic.

26 HOW 'THE ROOM' RELATES TO CREATIVITY

1 – Tommy is an artist, albeit an extreme one, and he gave himself permission to create.

2 – His self-belief was rock-solid, enough to ignore the masses and persist no matter what.

3 – While you win some and lose some, you can try again. Next time you'll fail less. If you're anything like Tommy Wiseau and other creative people, you will keep working.

4 – With the help of his friend, Tommy gave himself permission to accept The Room for what it was: not a powerful romantic drama but a whole other kind of entertainment, unique and valuable in its own way.

5 – When we take the first step to create, we find passion in our work, the kind of passion that drives us to push on, no matter what. We discover persistence.

6 - Whatever we create today, it will never be as 'bad' as The

Room.

Failing helps. Read this again: failing helps.

Helping you is why failure exists. It is its reason for being. Failing forces you to see things in a different light. It forces you to try again, sometimes repeatedly. The next time you try, you'll fail less. The next time, things will be better; the next time, better again. Failing forces you to try different ways until you find the way that works.

Keep going.

Keep 'failing' until you are producing something you are happy with.

Activity 8: Worst writing ever!

Create something awful. Please. You can do it. You're a terrible writer, you say? Great, you're perfect for the job!

Write the worst bit of writing ever. It can be a short poem or a song, a rhyme or a saucy limerick, five lines of a short story, melodramatic dialogue straight out of daytime soap opera, or anything else you fancy. You decide.

But be sure to make it AWFUL.

Off-key. Off-colour. Spelling mistakes. Bad grammar.

Make it the complete opposite of what it 'should' be.

Here's mine:

Been awake with your papers and my thoughts and your casseroles have me vomiting the rest of the time. Oh hello sunchine. Hello halo. Please praise me. I've got much to say.

I'm sure that given time, I can come up with better (I mean, worse… ugh, you know what I'm trying to say).

Your turn. Grab your writer's permit while you can, and give it a try.

Fail big, okay?

27 FEEL THE FEAR AND THROW UP ANYWAY

How scared are you of taking your first step? Use my very scientific scale of 0-10 where 0 is throwing caution to the wind and 10 is throwing up until you clog up the toilet (sorry).

Meet some folks you know who score an easy 10.

1. Henry Fonda (1905-1982).

Henry Fonda was an American actor from Nebraska. He had debilitating stage fright. Over five decades of professional acting, he confessed to feeling utterly miserable before walking on to a stage or set. The fear was so bad in fact that before every single performance, he threw up.

How did he get past the fear?

Henry soon realised that in order to do what he loved (acting), he would have to make some adjustments. He would have to do what he had to do, like keeping a bucket in the wings. Like telling himself he'd be okay. Like reminding himself that nothing else on earth could rival the thrill of acting.

So before stepping onto a set or stage, Henry would throw up, wipe his mouth, and go on. Once he made a start, his fear receded and he finished the performance. He relied on this method for every single performance, and each job he completed brought more work his way. He quickly came to be regarded as a sought-after talent, despite the pre-performance nerves that dogged his entire professional career. As much as fear made him nauseous to the point of vomiting, Henry made sure to be just as persistent, using his bucket trick time and time again.

2. Adele (1988 – present)

Adele Adkins is from London, England. Money was tight in her one-parent family. She and her mother worked hard and sacrificed greatly to pay for the piano and voice lessons that enabled Adele to record her unique voice and lyrics. She has managed to work professionally since her teens.

Adele suffers considerable performance-related anxiety. She says that before a show she'll moan and complain, she gets fidgety, she tries to escape or get out of having to do it. Despite this, she continues to write and perform the songs that bring her happiness and success.

3. Yours truly (1976 – present)

I am a daughter, a sister, a wife, a mother to two children, and a writer. I draft pieces for publication, pitch my ideas for fiction and non-fiction, and submit deeply personal work for publication.

I have suffered with anxiety since childhood. Then and now, my hands and feet sweat profusely whenever I have to face anything new. Whenever I know I have to shake hands, my hands and feet sweat so much they drip. They swell up. They stay swollen, cold, and clammy for hours.

At seventeen, I left home for college in Dublin, coming home on weekends for a night or two. During that first year, I would wake every Sunday morning and spend the day nauseous and miserable, before throwing up and getting the bus back to the capital.

Recently, to promote a workshop I was teaching, I had a radio interview, an in-person thing with a fabulous DJ at my local station. For days leading up to it, I wrestled with excuses that I might use to get out of it:

My car's run out of diesel;

My son is covered in angry red spots;

There's a family emergency and I'm needed immediately.

But I had a full tank of fuel. My kids were well and gone to school. No phone calls had come through necessitating a frenzied drive to my hometown. Instead, with a dry flannel facecloth on the passenger seat, I drove to the radio station. I walked in, we shook hands, my sweaty hand in her dry warm one and I gave an interview I was proud of.

It didn't stop the fear though. I'd told the venue that I was expecting 12 attendees. I convinced myself that I could deal with 15 if the demand was there. I needn't have fretted. A week to go and there were zero signups. Then in 24 hours, I got two. That's more like it I thought, and I spent a little money on social media advertising. That got me… a third signup.

Three people didn't even cover my costs. My ego was desperate for more, and my brain reminded me that I was making a loss.

For days before the workshop, I kept hoping things would happen to stop me. Things that I could say were outside of my control, things that I could justifiably use to cancel or at least postpone the workshop (and the accompanying dread). I thanked the heavens (literally): that week brought a heavy storm, causing severe weather warnings right across the country. This was wonderful: workshoppers might have to navigate difficult roads. I could get stuck in a flood en route. Or a tree could have fallen on the venue and gallons and gallons of rainwater could be pouring in while I daydreamed. I could cancel the whole thing.

Alas, the storms abated and the warnings were lifted. But that didn't stop me.

The morning of the workshop, I kept checking my youngest son, convinced that he was coming down with something and that I should stay home. My husband, sick sore and tired of my fretting, reminded me that time waits for no woman, and pushed me firmly toward the front door, saying things like 'go' and 'start the engine' and 'now'…

There was no getting out of it. I had to turn up. So I did. My three attendees and I met in Drogheda's Barbican Centre and we spent the day exploring the best way for these ordinary people to claim back their creative selves. It went well. In fact, it was fantastic. Some things went well and there was a hiccup or two, but I came home feeling thrilled, fulfilled, and incredibly proud of myself and my work.

See how anxiety tricked me? It does the same to us all. It's toxic and it's powerful, but the antidote is always the same: do your thing.

Keep turning up, keep doing your thing. As per me, Laurence, and a lot of other people:

'You either battle or walk away.' Laurence Olivier, actor, director.

'Lots and lots of things scare me; but you just get on with it. Fear can transform into petrol. I get stage fright all the time; the more I act the more I feel it. But you just have to use it to your advantage.' Judi Dench, actor

'You just have to throw yourself onstage.' John Simm, actor, director.

28 TRICK THE TRICKSTER

This part isn't about getting through fear exactly. I think the best we can do is 'disarm' fear long enough to get started on the thing we want to do. Disarming fear involves taking anxiety on at its own game and coming up with your own tricks.

Like Henry and his bucket, I've got a few tricks of my own:

On writing days, I remind myself that when I was on the 'not writing' route, I was safe but miserable. I was angry and afraid and deeply unhappy.

On deadline days, I tell myself that once I get down the bones of a piece, I won't feel the fear so much, there's a little relief in its place. Experience reassures me that the fear fades, moves into the background, until tomorrow when it rises and roars at me again.

On days when writing allergies are acute, I tell myself I've only to work for 15 minutes. When time's up, the allergies have subsided, and I keep typing.

On teaching days, I drive to the venue and spend a few minutes in the parking lot with the music maxed out—Foo Fighters are best for pure unadulterated energy but in a pinch Wham! will do.

On occasions where I've lost money, I evaluate what I gained. Running that workshop gave me:

Confidence;

Three new contacts;

The knowledge that I can do it;

The reassurance that the material worked, that my ideas, my teaching, helped other people.

Hooray! I'd take all of those things any day.

I forgive myself the loss of the money, stop and think, and plan to do it better next time. Steps I can take to make sure I lose less money, or make a profit:

Seek out funding;

Advertise more;

Change my format (from workshop to the book you're holding in your hand).

On days when I have to meet new people in a professional context, I remind myself of the things I'm good at: connecting with strangers and putting them at their ease. I use my warm friendly manner to give a sense of openness to the people I'm meeting. It's my way of asking them to trust me, asking them to be themselves just enough to get something useful out of the day. It is my way of reassuring them that good enough is good enough, and that we are all human. No one has to be right or correct or perfect.

I also bring a dry flannel facecloth to dry my hands with, an extra shirt, and lots of deodorant.

Activity 9:

What can you do to get through the nerves? Think of things that might aid you in doing what you fear doing. It might be something practical or sensory. It might be a ritual, a prayer or a phrase that helps you. Here are a few prompts to help you start.

I could use

____

____

I could think of

____

____

I could ask for

____

____

I could do

____

____

29 ALL TALK

Remember back at the start, when I introduced myself? I told you that I am a strong person, but I also love making plans then tell other people about the plan.

Sometimes I go back to the plan and 'replan' the plan. I love replanning the plan. It means I can go and tell the first lot of people, and then tell the second lot of people....

As a kid, I was confident and smart. When I was nine, I read from the pulpit at mass. Later, on the way home, a woman told me and my mother how well I'd done. She couldn't believe I was 'Only nine years old?' Well I can tell you, I was thrilled. In school, I always managed to ace things like spellings and English. On Fridays when we did spelling tests, I grinned like a Cheshire cat.

Then I got to high school and some folks in my town dreamed up a stage show, a big retro musical thing that the whole community could audition for. It was exciting and pretty cool and all us teenagers were eager to get a part. But I wasn't interested in being a Beatle, Sandy Shaw, Frida or Agnetha.

I had a talent. They'd told me when I was nine that I read nicely, I spoke nicely, and I was confident. So, I decided there and then that I was going to be the voice of the show. Nothing but narrator would do. Leave it to me to be the glue between The Beatles and the BeeGees, the Bay City Rollers and Ziggy Stardust, 80s Bowie and Wham!

My friends were sure I'd get it and told me so. Feigning indifference was hard when I couldn't manage to think of anything else. I gave a good audition and started to believe my friends were right.

A few days later came the news – they wanted me as narrator.

So I took it, right?

Wrong.

There was a rush of emotions as I took in their offer, another rush as I refused. I shrugged as friends wanted to know why I wasn't taking the role, and the reason sprang forth: the Inter cert. These were the State-set exams, half way through high school.

Not important, just incredibly convenient.

My best friend begged me to reconsider my decision. She was upset that she would have to go and rehearse in the town's old cinema for weeks without me. But refusing the role meant being in demand so to speak, and that gave me more pleasure than reading lines for any show. What a problem it was being great enough at everything that I had to choose one braggable thing over another braggable thing! This was going to be epic!

The role of narrator was offered to the next person, a girl from my class, because the show must go on. But on opening night (I managed to take time out of my busy revision schedule to buy a ticket, just to be supportive…), every word Suzette read out had me seething, thinking to myself that not only would I have done it better, I was obviously the only one in this class who's taking the exams seriously!

After a week (okay, two or three months), the jealousy subsided; I had my exams as distraction, and the promise of some glorious grades. Getting good grades and praise for them was worth more to me than the unknown unquantified narrator's role in a small town show, a role whose success is relative. But an A minus or a B plus—now they are easy to measure.

I told myself that I could have taken either path; both would have brought me praise and glory, and boy did I love that feeling. I traded on it for years until an old school friend inadvertently made me check myself.

I knew Jackie from school, so when we reconnected on Facebook a few years ago, I learned that she followed her dream: she trained in acting and film and enjoys a successful career as a film editor. Hooray, I thought, how exciting. It is always a thrill to see people do what they love and are good at.

So Jackie posts online about a film she's just finished: in this instance, she also narrated the piece she edited. So being supportive, I write 'Well done, especially on the narration… It's on my list of 'things to do in life' ha ha… Any day now…' I tapped the 'Send' button and bit my lip. I told myself I was happy for her, did a little non-combative comparison of the two of us for an hour or so, and proceeded to gently seethe for the rest of the day.

I would've been fine; I was on the mend until I read her reply: 'Thanks, it was good fun. And you will do it some day if you really want I'm sure!'

A sudden light shone, and it hurt.

Like a fox about to be caught, I was running from the henhouse without a kill. I tumbled back to my den and declared to the others that the henhouse was empty. Until I noticed the chicken feathers in the fur of my peers. They'd been in the henhouse, they'd seen the birds, and had sated themselves.

I'd been caught. All talk. All talk with neither trousers nor shirt nor underwear.

I burned with anger and retorted (to Facebook) 'I really DO want, you better BET I want.' What had made me so angry? Someone fulfilling her potential? Someone doing what she wants to do? Someone sacrificing time, money, and energy to be trained and ready to answer opportunity's knock?

At the time, I didn't know what was making me so angry, bar the perceived audacity of a woman I'd not seen in years. So I spent the next week spiralling into unexplained crankiness, barking at the kids for the slightest thing, burning the dinner more often than usual, dropping things, running out of things, and making zero progress on anything. To hell with work, I decided, all bared teeth and rant. The house and my writing could wait. My usual mindful parenting sat ignored while I bashed around the house telling myself that this was totally unfair, she'd just gone and done something cool, while here I was waiting for the right time, the right everything. Didn't she know that I wanted to be the one narrating? Narrating her project, the show twenty years ago, and every damn thing in between.

I raged in the drama, immersed myself in anger that burned me to a crisp. I knew it was just desserts, but every ounce of energy was focussed on the words of a person I hadn't seen in decades, and her supposed audacity at doing something I'd always believed—no, I'd always said—I would do.

My mind went off on tangents. Was she trained? Probably not, I told myself. She probably just did it, just like that, and the thought of it made me furious. Maybe she had trained as an actor, but it probably was some two-bit school.

'Was it RADA darling? Was it? No, I didn't think so.'

If she'd sacrificed, if she'd worked for it, I didn't care. I couldn't see any evidence of anything except someone snatching away what was rightfully mine…

Wait a minute. Back up.

See those defences rack up? Quick and efficient! Such drama! Such melodrama.

Distract distract distract. Anything to stop myself from facing reality. 'I've not done it, I had the chance to do it, and I blew it. And it still bothers me.' (sticks fingers in ears and sings lalalalalalah).

Oh yes, I was angry. Angry as a woman who couldn't avoid looking at the truth any longer.

The truth being that I had my chance and I didn't take it. Worse again, here I was twenty years later, still talking about what Big Ole Important Me was going to do, and doing nothing about it.

For the record, Jackie didn't just 'go and do' anything. Like many people working in film, she trained in acting (yes, in a great school), worked her socks off, and spent time and money honing her skills. She applied for jobs in the industry, got known for working hard and producing good stuff, which led to more jobs.

So when one job needs a narrator, and there's Jackie: trained, ready, with an absolutely rocking speaking voice...

Seriously. If I'd slowed down enough to notice, I'd have realised all this instead of jumping to conclusions. I'd have sensed my own resentment and hopefully would have done something about it.

It's not that I'm jealous of someone else (that's a bit of a lie. Jackie's voice is completely rocking). It's that I'm angry with myself.

For not doing what I said I'd do. For talking in the first place.

I'm all talk. I'm crap. I'll just shut up in future.

Pause: this is Resistance in all its finery. It builds up this phenomenal argument as to why you should just stick a nice big cross into the dirt, climb up on it and live there wailing for all eternity. I'd gotten comfortable on my cross. I didn't have to do anything, just look out over the horizon, give the odd wail, look good. It was glorious.

But the world doesn't want me stuck in the dirt, and it can see the sulk behind the smile. The world needs me to do, to create. To give colour and flavour to my life and the lives of others.

The point is this: you'll do it someday if you really want to, just like Jackie said. She was sure of it. And she's right. If I really wanted to, I could do it. Do whatever it takes to get the job. Voice training, acting, or just sticking my hand up and saying 'I'll do it, now, for free. Now giz a job!'

You can stay on your cross or get off it. But make no mistake: the choice is yours, nobody else's. And you don't have the right to go blaming others for choosing to do what they did.

Honestly, I kinda still want to narrate, but I also want to do it all, and I can't. I just can't. Instead, I live with my choices and I decide to be kind about them. Sometimes, like this time, I work hard to find the worth in them, and I make plans to help me not mess up again.

For the record, our online conversation continued a bit longer. I told Facebook, Jackie, and the world (but of course!) that I would tackle narration some day, and that it would help if I finished my edits first.

Her reply was supportive: 'Keep at it.'

So I do. And I know that if and when I do the narration thing, she'll be one of the first people I'll contact. Thanks Jackie.

30 I'LL TELL YOU WHAT I WANT! WHAT I REALLY REALLY WANT!

Jackie is the kind of professional who is serious about the job, serious enough to invest time and energy into training. And she is successful at that job. Once I understood my own story, saw my own naked begrudgery of both her seriousness and her success, it made me stop and think.

What do I actually want? Do I want to be a narrator? And did those original whispers come from myself or from somebody else?

I realise that I want what I'd always wanted: a family, a business, good health, dark chocolate. And would you look at that, I have it in spades. Bar the chocolate.

The truth is, I also want to narrate. Sort of. Not a lot. Just a little. Wanting a little of everything is okay, isn't it? Isn't it? Okay, so I'm human and therefore forgivable.

What I really want is to forgive myself and my insecurities. I'm not seeking total absolution, just enough to let me do the things I really want to do. Start the books, write the books, untangle the messy middles, clean up the crappy ends, and publish them in print and audio.

Hey, maybe I will need a narrator after all.

Activity 10:

A note before you start: This activity is not meant to affront. Please know that it is no failure to throw something to the side if you decide it is definitely not 'you'. Don't worry about saving face. It's just you and me remember? So be faithful to yourself. Take the time now to think through what is important to you, not anyone else.

A useful rule of thumb is this: if you would do it for free, it's important.

1. Think of the creative thing you'd like to do. Did it start as someone else's goal and somehow become yours?

____

____

____

2. Ask yourself how much you want it.

____

____

____

3. Remember the last time someone said to you 'You'd be great at

(such and such)'? What was your gut reaction? Does it tie in with your goals for yourself?

PART THREE: DOING

'Thinking will not overcome fear, but action will.'
  W. CLEMENT STONE
  AMERICAN BUSINESSMAN

31 MIND THE GAP

One activity I love for myself and others is writing from a prompt: using a picture or a sentence to trigger a new idea, then writing for a few minutes to see what comes out of you and where it goes.

There was one such time I prepared prompts, and gave the slips of paper out to a group of workshoppers. As most people chewed on a pencil, wrote down their first sentence, or scribbled something only to scrawl a line through it, one woman seemed to not do anything. She seemed to be paused, her face frozen tight, the cool ice of panic in her eyes, and I realised she had slipped into the gap.

The gap is that moment between the excitement of starting and the dawn of blankness as your mind empties clean out. I'd forgotten to warn my colleague about the gap and she'd fallen in.

While others around you are busy scribbling down what you imagine to be genius words or other deep and meaningfuls, you sit there feeling like the class dunce and willing the panic to back off. You are supposed to be writing, aren't you? You try to think through your five Ws? Or is it only four? Let's see, first comes 'what', then 'where'. No, it's 'why'. Isn't it 'why'? Wait, what was the first one again?

I fought the urge to stand up and walk over to her, tell her how to start, help her to brainstorm. Instead, I looked down, started writing something, anything, just to give her space and time.

The gap lasts only a second or two, but in our heads, it feels like an eternity. It's like everyone else is up and at it while you're being pulled down a chasm of pathetic. It's like all eyes are on you, waiting for you to perform, to deliver, to somehow instinctively know the answers, and to get them right first time. But your paper is still as blank as it's always been while others are still scribbling. Time will soon be up and you're sure you'll be sat there like an idiot.

It happens in all creative pursuits: you dump some clay on your potter's wheel and wonder how to turn the thing. Your dancing troupe bustles you onstage where your feet suddenly freeze. The bread recipe you've made a million times mocks you like a ghost you can't quite see.

But when I looked up again, her pen was moving. Hallelujah, I thought, praising her strength and all the writing gods. I went round the group one by one; those who wanted to read their work could do so, and this woman was last.

'How did you find the exercise?' I asked her. She found it difficult she said, she struggled to make a start and felt panic especially as others were already making progress while she stared at empty lines.

I wanted to know how she got over the gap.

"I had one word," she told us. "It was nothing really but I put it down, and that was my start." She proceeded to read out a strong and touching few lines, made all the more poignant by the pain that bore it.

We all feel the gap sometimes. Some of us feel it every single time we go to the desk or the stage or the potter's wheel. Where do I start? Where will this end?

Don't worry about the destination, just take the first step and mind the gap.

SAFE HANDS

32 WE ARE NOT ALONE

Many people have become more creative in their daily lives and the world didn't stop turning. Countless other people who are just like you have taken the first steps toward making space and time for themselves, to do the things that make them happy.

The dentist who plays jazz piano on a Thursday night; the programmer who flies a single engine Cessna at the weekends; the nurse who writes for an hour on her commute; the teacher who crochets for 10 minutes before the kids barrel in for the day; the engineer who gets to his quarry site at dawn to photograph sunrise over the hills; the customer service agent who's writing his own short film with plans to direct; the civil servant who paints oils onto canvas. These are all real people whose lives and wellbeing are enriched by using their hands for something easy and fun. Some publicise what they do, others just do and are content with that.

Permission to do your creative thing comes from no one but you. It is a choice you have, and will always have.

Fear is always there. It is there for you and it is there for me. Some of us show it, some of us hide it, but it is real and it is persistent. Make peace with this fact and know that you are not alone.

Who says the factory worker can't learn the fiddle? Who's allowed stop the nurse from writing poetry or auditioning for a part in a play? Who gets to say whether you're entitled to your thing? Who gets to say that you deserve it? Who gets to say you are good enough at the activity to 'justify' spending time on it?

It's not about earning the right. It's not about deserving the time. It's not about talent or glory.

It's about using your own safe hands.

By claiming time for yourself, you're quietly and safely challenging this incorrect belief about yourself. You are taking control of your wellbeing. By reading this and doing even one activity, you've taken your first step.

Congratulations.

33 TRAINEE DALAI LAMA

Now, I did promise there'd be no Dalai Lama sayings. For one thing, I don't know much about faith or religion. For another, his turns of phrases are way cooler than mine.

The Dalai Lama is big into compassion, but my specialist subject is harshness. Specifically: harshness towards myself. I'll not go into it, but suffice it to say that I treated myself badly for years, I took small steps that became giant leaps, and found that kinder is nicer. The Dalai Lama would agree however that now, more than ever, adults need self-compassion.

Self-compassion made a late appearance in my life, and probably tied in with becoming a parent. Kids are absolute f*ckers. Sorry, but they are. Their very existence forces lazy sods like me to do everything we spent years happily ignoring, like facing up to responsibility, watching our money, or being patient. Wiping, praising, feeding, feeding, praising, wiping. There is something life-changing about shaking your kid's faeces into a toilet bowl, prising human waste from their teeny tiny clothing.

For this (and for many other reasons), children are in my opinion worth it. All this work is not really their doing and so I have learned to forgive and love the people they are. It felt good to take them as they are, so I tried it on myself. By doing creative things and not flagellating myself if it wasn't right or cool or perfect, I found the person inside that I still am. The more I practise this, the easier it gets.

Like parenting, self-compassion has not come easy to me. I was angry for a long time until I'd had enough of being my own punchbag; but I still struggled: treating myself with care felt like indulgence. I had to go read some of Dr. Kristin Neff's books and articles to learn what self-compassion really was.

It's taken me a long time to find myself and my creativity. I constantly forget to mind myself and my well-being. But I am getting there. I am more tuned into the whispers, more forgiving of the roars, and I know that when I feel a struggle inside of me, it's usually Resistance in one form or another. At its most basic, Resistance wins when we stay put, when we admit that the hill is too steep and we should quit. We can slow down, we can turn back and get help, we can plan better or rest and train. Remember that for many of us, self-compassion is a traineeship, and we are absolutely allowed baby steps.

But do nothing? Go home and never come back? Can you really do that?

I'd love nothing more than to quit writing, stop creating. Writing is hard. Often I wish the first draft would be enough. My work gets rejected a lot and I sometimes feel that it's me personally who's failed. That is one of the many thousands of reasons we think we should stop trying.

But will it stop the fire burning inside? People the world over have tried ignoring it and they never manage to snuff it out. Ignoring it only makes it burn longer and harder until it eats away at us from the inside.

Those who fight it are never happy, and I have proved that to myself time after time.

There's no easy way to work out which thoughts are fear talking to us and which thoughts are our own. You must tune in and listen to how it sounds. If it's bringing you closer to where you truly want to be, it's probably your own wisdom. Try something on, see what comes, all while proving to yourself that doing so will not cause the sky to fall in.

And if the sky does fall in, just drop me a mail with concrete data-based scientific evidence certified by a senior geophysicist to obtain a full refund of your book purchase.

NOTES ON THIS CHAPTER:

Dr. Kristin Neff has written a great article 'The 5 Myths of Self-Compassion'. For the link to this, go to my website www.nikkiweston.com/safe-hands-recommended-reading

Activity 11:

1. What does your creative outlet, your 'need to do', tell you?

____

____

____

2. What does fear reply with? Is it accurate?

____

____

____

3. When in the past has your 'need to do' been RIGHT?

____

____

____

4. Knowing all this, I can now tell my 'need-to-do' the following:

____

____

____

34 BREAKING THE RULES

I made a note to myself to think hard about the end section of this book. I guess I thought I needed to leave you with something, like a motivational prompt such as 'now go do it!' or 'what's stopping you?' Writers like me are often advised to check in at the end of a book such as this, and ask readers the question 'has this book helped you?' Like we can somehow measure whether or not there's been an improvement.

I gave some thought too to writing a kind of quiz, a 'before and after' questionnaire thingey that would help you figure out if your life has gotten better since you read the book. Truth be told, I want to do this. My ego is wanting proof that this book is worthy of your time and attention. It's also wanting to get your approval and maybe a nice book review somewhere.

Sometimes, writers are told to 'reiterate the stuff we talked about in the introduction,' like completing the conceptual circle or something. But instead I'm going to do the 'before and after' thingey with myself and ask myself did I achieve what I set out to do? This was my project after all; creative recovery and well-being has been important to me for the last few years; telling others about my recovery so they may recover themselves became the goal of this book. That aim has become my obsession, I admit, to the point where I've woken at 5am and start scribbling stuff in the dark.

My goal in *Safe Hands* is important to me. Did I give my ideas clearly and honestly and tell others what it's like to be nauseous and do stuff anyway, sharing my living experiences? Did I keep the various activities and discussions simple and accessible so that you, dear reader, might start on your creativity?

I know my intentions were good and I trust these hands of mine. I know that together we did the best we could. I could spend another month or two fixing and tweaking and adding to the manuscript, but good enough is good enough and I bet the Dalai Lama would agree.

35 AND NOW...

Well done on reading and thinking. Well done on doing the activities. Well done on feeling silly and squirmy and guilty and weird. You really are in the best of hands.

Your job is this:

make a little time for your creative recovery.
Turn up,
tune in,
and do.

Do one small thing on your chosen creative pursuit. If you're wanting to try stand-up, all that friend of a friend who runs an open mic night. If you yearn to paint, go buy a cheap-as-chips beginners' set of acrylics or watercolours. If you think you could teach yoga, talk to whoever instructs you. Can they recommend a training college?

How much can you expect to pay?

If it scares you a little, that's okay. If it scares you to paralysis, it could be that it's too big. Easy, just make it smaller. Keep making it smaller until the fear is so small you can't see it anymore. It's still there, just harder to see.

Activity 12:

One step I can take this week is:

____

____

____

One step I can take this month is:

____

____

____

One step I can take this year is:

____

____

____

Keep inching forward, keep making mistakes. You're in safe hands.

36 SAFE DATES

An Artist's Date is a concept that comes from Julia Cameron's 12-week program 'The Artist's Way'. It is that chunk of time you make for yourself where you do something fun. It can be fifteen minutes, an hour, or the entire day. Small and accessible means it will probably fit easily into our lives.

It can be anything you like: an excursion, a quick splash of poster paints on the back of butcher paper, learning the foxtrot. Buying knitting needles and some yarn and using YouTube to reacquaint yourself with plain and purl; planting a row of cabbages; snipping a handful of wildflowers, arranging them in a pretty bottle, maybe photographing them, printing it big and bold at the print shop and framing it while you're there!

Do your thing your way: Think of the kid you were; what does s/he like to do for the sheer fun of it? Children are neither serious nor high-brow and they're generally happy to do things that are low cost or free.

Keep it fun. Make it cheap.

Try and do it alone; don't make plans to meet anyone else there. Having someone else there makes us self-conscious or afraid of looking silly. It also leaves us unable to fully focus on the task in hand, and in some cases if we are trying to impress another person, we don't have the time or brain space to fully immerse ourselves into the activity.

Give yourself permission if you need to. There is neither right nor wrong. Have faith for a little while and enjoy the doing.

Below are some easy and cheap tools that you can use to reclaim time to yourself. Remember: "process versus product" (i.e. it's the process of creating rather than the resulting product that makes us feel good).

Here are some ideas to get you started:

- Take a walk to a park or the countryside.

- Buy a cheap sketchpad in the supermarket or hobby shop, then sit on a park bench or beach and doodle for a while. Who gives a sh!t who's watching; get started and get lost ;-)

- Stop by a 'retro' sweetshop for a quarter-pound of your favourite childhood sweets.

- Head to a nearby bay or harbour and photograph the boats.

- Go to a charity shop and buy something that catches your eye. I did this once, buying an old canvas print for €3 that appealed to me. This became my first artist date. A month or so later, I went to the *Art and Hobby* shop and bought a beginner's set of cheap acrylics for under €10 (another artist date). I made a third artist date about a month later, pulled out my wee beginner's set of paints and did an hour's touch-up at the kitchen table. Breaking up a project in this way makes it less overwhelming and therefore much more likely to get done.

- Hop on a local tourist bus and see what the visitors see.

- Visit a haberdashery shop and look at the range of ribbons, buttons, and fabrics.

- Visit a local garden centre and pick up a new plant for your office or bedroom.

- Go to a local gallery for a browse and a coffee.

- Catch a local play or musical. Check out your local amateur dramatics theatre for shows.

- Movie solitude: one evening, I was crankier than usual and knew an artist date was well overdue. Worse, I was so irritable I didn't want to leave the house or plan anything too taxing, and just needed to be at home. So I sent the kids off with the husband, got a blanket, some tea and chocolate, and I browsed through Netflix. 'Big Eyes' with Amy Adams and Christoph Waltz is a drama biography of US artist Margaret Keane's life and work as she escapes a nasty husband and a very big lie.

- Collage at home: You'll need a glue stick like Pritt stick, a sheet of paper or card, and an old magazine. Cut up a few magazine pages, and get sticking! Work without thinking for 5 or 10 minutes until the paper is covered with old bits. This is my go-to artist date when I'm pushed for time or when I'm furious at everything. Keep the leftover bits of magazine cuts in a clear punch pocket for next time.

- Leaf rubbing: Autumn is a time for casting off the old, so grab some leaves, crayons and paper, and do a leaf-rubbing and pretend that you're five years old again.

- Check out local art groups on Facebook. Mine is the *Dublin Sketchers* group. Every Sunday, this group of people go to a different part of Dublin city, sketch whatever they see for an hour, then meet for coffee or a pint and swap sketch books. I did it once, it was huge fun and I met some lovely people.

SAFE DATES BY ACTIVITY:

Below are a few more ideas, ordered by profession. They're super-basic, so playing with these will allow you safely explore stuff without having to launch into A Commitment. There are no rules, only guidelines.

These activities exercise (exorcise?) our expectations of ourselves, relaxing the pressure to perform, or to get it right. These steps are completely disposable and hurt no one.

You might feel uncomfortable at first, but stick with it. You only get better at something by doing, and we all start somewhere.

Artist

- Buy some cheap student paints and using the brush inside the set, paint the top flaps of a cereal box. Slide the inner sleeve of cereal back into the box. Yes, it's silly. That's the point.

Comedian

- Remember a bad joke, one that's overused and clichéd; write it down. Then rewrite it fresher and better.

- Look in the mirror and imagine you're a wildlife expert narrating yourself eating your breakfast

Essayist

- Look around you. What is your body touching? Butt on a chair or bench? Feet on carpet? Take one of the things you're in contact with and write 6 sentences about its invention. One sentence each for the what, the which, the where, the who, the why, and the how. It doesn't have to be true or accurate, no research is needed.

Musician

- Get a clean comb (hard to find, I know) and some paper, wrap the comb and hum.

- If you hate your singing voice, get a second-hand mouth-organ in a charity shop, and pretend you're playing the blues.

- Go to your music collection and find the album you like the least. Play one song from it.

Photography

- If you have a smartphone, turn on the camera and take selfies that no one will ever see. Delete same (or not!).

- If you don't have a smartphone, buy a disposable camera and shoot stuff around your home.

Playwright

- Stick a sock on your hand and act out a scene from the last movie you saw.

- Choose any of the following prompts and write a short scene:

- A young woman pushing a pram feels the swoop of a bird overhead.

- You're driving past a lake at night and suddenly a child walks out of the woods onto the road.

- The radio announces that there's an outbreak of smallpox detected in your neighbourhood.

- You make a cup of coffee, and no matter how you try, the sugar slides down the outside of the cup.

- On the way home from work, you pick up a newspaper. Your photograph is front page, and the headline reads 'Wanted!'

- A man awakes in an Amazonian rainforest with a moving bulldozer only yards away

- Television has been invented but it hasn't occurred to anyone that a colour one might be nice.

- You are an artist and the colour yellow has never existed.

- You are a time-travelling farmer and you find a trail of blood leading to a silo.

- You are a mouse who looks in a mirror and finds you're a cat.

- You are a rubik's cube and the only person who can solve you is you.

- You are the last eagle in a valley of predators.

- You are the cue caller on opening night but none of the cast has turned up. Suddenly the ghosts of great actors like Humphrey Bogart and Lauren Bacall turn up instead. Will the show go on?

- You wake up on D-day and find your surname is Hitler.

Storytelling

- Back to the socks! The holier the better! Tell a story from a famous character's point of view. It can be MacBeth in a Highlands castle or Oscar the Grouch in his trash can. It doesn't matter. What matters is the doing.

- Turn on the radio and listen to the accent of the next person talking. Nab that accent and narrate out loud whatever it is you're doing. The dishes in a Scottish lilt, driving the kids to music pretending you're from New Zealand.

Remember! Creativity is:

'-' less about changing your self

'+' more about nurturing the person you are.

P.S. It's cheaper than therapy…

37 ENJOYED SAFE HANDS?

Then tell your friends, leave a review online, or just keep in touch!

Part of the reason I write books is to connect with people. It's wonderful to help others, and I want to reach as many people as possible. Honestly would love to hear how you've been getting on, even if you've not managed to do anything yet. Or maybe especially.

Sign up to my quarterly newsletter for updates, exclusive free essays, and news on releases and events:

http://www.nikkiweston.com

This is where you'll also find printable workbooks, resources, and free content.

My website also has a 'Recommended Reading' section. I put it over there on purpose, I don't want it to be a barrier to your doing. So do yourself a favour, leave the recommended reading for a decade or two, and go have fun instead.

Make some pizza dough.

Set up a Men's Shed.

Wear your favourite hat and talk like Audrey Hepburn in 'My Fair Lady'.

If you think the *Safe Hands* concept can help others, please tell your friends about the book and the thinking behind it. And if you could swing it, I'd appreciate a review on the book platform you purchased *Safe Hands* from. Being self-published, my reputation may be built by me, but it can only be sustained by you.

Thank you for your time reading *Safe Hands*. I don't have all the answers, but I had a ball writing it for you. It is my way of supporting myself: using my potential, making decisions, looking at the options available to me, and exercising a few of them. I always did agree with Robert DeNiro: when someone remarked that he was a great talent, he replied, 'The talent is in the choices'.

Wishing you and your creative future all the very best.

Nikki Weston

ABOUT THE AUTHOR

Nikki Weston lives in Dublin, Ireland, with her family. She writes freelance articles, long and short fiction, and self-publishes non-fiction on the parts of ourselves we'd rather hide. 'Safe Hands' is her first non-fiction book.

Nikki loves to hear from readers, so join her over on the 'Safe Hands' Facebook page: https://www.facebook.com/Safe-Hands-100718164713393/?modal=admin_todo_tour

To get her quarterly newsletter for news and bonus essays, sign up at http://www.nikkiweston.com/